Who's a *Chatty* Boy Then?

Choosing a suitable budgerigar and teaching it to talk

Elizabeth Wright

Four Times Champion
Talking Bird Trainer

Who's a Chatty Boy Then?

First published in the UK in January 2015 by MyVoice Publishing

Copyright: © Elizabeth Wright

Elizabeth Wright asserts the moral right to be identified as the author of this work

Published by: MyVoice Publishing,

www.myvoicepublishing.co.uk

ISBN: 978-1-909359-49-9

Contents

Who's a Chatty Boy Then?

Foreword

Elizabeth Wright writes excellent work, both comedy and historical fact (MyVoice published 'Belle Tout, The little lighthouse that moved' in 2013)

When I found out more about Elizabeth's background and expertise, I asked her to write a book about the astonishing results she experienced in teaching budgerigars to talk. To write the book to educate and enable others to achieve the same levels of success. This book is the result.

Extracting information from her is hard work due to her natural modesty. Slowly, the depth of her knowledge and experience is revealed and it seems to be never-ending, more impressive as our conversations evolve.

I knew that she appeared on the television and that she won the Talking Bird Competition at the National Exhibition of Cage Birds four times, but didn't realise the number of birds that she achieved this with as well as how many runners up prizes she won. One year she managed a clean sweep with the top 3 places. I am not sure whether she stopped competing because it was no longer a challenge or perhaps to give the other competitors a chance!

Elizabeth was a noted breeder and exhibitor of Budgerigars, as well as a monthly contributor of an advice column to Pet Product Marketing for eleven years. This magazine was distributed to the pet trade and allied traders - in other words she advised the experts. In addition she wrote literally hundreds of articles for various bird magazines around the globe – proving that she is not just a British expert, but worldwide. Elizabeth is recognised for her expertise and experience in Australia and America as well.

After she stopped competing with her own birds, she became an acclaimed steward for the International

Ornithological Association, conveying British entries to World Bird Shows. She was the number one person that Television companies went to when they needed a genuine talking bird trainer. or indeed a bird expert. on their shows for many years. She and her birds were in great demand by advertisers and you may have seen her in past appearances.

We have persuaded her to write this guide, and I cannot think of a better of more highly qualified person to do so.

I wish you luck with the training of your Budgerigar!

Rex Sumner
MyVoice Publishing Ltd

Introduction

The perky budgerigar is a member of the talkative parrot family and its intelligence and 'ego' personality play a great part in making it the world's third most popular pet, after dogs and cats.

Wild green specimens, then labelled Shell Parakeets or Australian Lovebirds, were brought to Europe from Australia in the 1840's by painter and ornithologist, John Gould. They have since established themselves as true family favourites, being inexpensive to buy and keep, are lovable, playful, chatty and entertaining. Not all budgerigars are suitable as talking pets so it makes sense to read all about them before you buy. Most importantly, spend time choosing one, especially as they can live 10 years or more.

Geoff Capes, one time world famous shot-put champion and the most capped British male athlete of all times, is an avid budgie breeder. As a past President of the Budgerigar Society and elected member of the BS General Council, he has this to say, "Budgies mimic more than they talk. You can start training them at six to eight weeks and how good they are isn't affected, as some people mistakenly believe, by their colour or sex."

Ryan Reynolds, from the Canadian Budgie Research Group made these illuminating comments in 2005: "I believe that science is finally starting to realise that birds are far more intelligent than anyone previously thought. Through understanding these parakeets, we are gaining valuable information about how they think and how we can provide them with a happier lifestyle. There has been an influx of published research demonstrating how much science has underestimated them. Until fairly recently scientists thought birds were not intelligent enough to use context when speaking... but under the right conditions, budgerigars are capable of not just speaking in context, but in extreme conversational language."

He went on to say that he believed budgies have always been able to communicate effectively with people, "It's just that we haven't been able to understand them. For the most part, budgies think humans are not smart enough to comprehend them, so they do not normally communicate in context with us. But once a bird realises that it can be understood, it tries much harder to converse. Budgies are social animals that can withdraw if they have no communication with other sentient beings. Once they know this is possible, they show an extreme enthusiasm to make it happen."

He strongly feels that the driving factor in establishing lines of communication between budgies and their owners is how well they bond with people and "how much they trust and love us. They often sense how we feel and think and ...their reward... is knowing that they are loved and are part of the family."

With 38 years of hands-on experience, of breeding, showing and selling budgerigars, especially for talking pets, and the owner of national prizewinning talking parrots, cockatoos and budgies, I can give you sound, practical advice to help you choose, tame and train your bird to talk.

There are no 100% guarantees that you will be the owner of a good talker; some individuals are more gifted than others, as humans can be at singing or playing the violin. The degree of success depends mostly on the trainer's input, which requires patience, persistence and a set routine coupled with an intelligent, responsive bird that has a good relationship with its owner. The budgie is a mimic, and vocalisation can occasionally be haphazard, such as the bird copying the ringtones of a phone or a dog barking, simply because it is attracted to these sounds. But the end result is all down to how much time, you, the owner and trainer, are prepared to give to making your pet budgie a gifted and entertaining talker.

The Author appearing on 'What's My Line'
with her two talking birds, Lulu and Cocky

Choosing Your Budgerigar

To start off the proper way, you need to look for a supplier of baby budgerigars and at the right time of the year.

The ideal age to buy your pet is around 6-8 weeks old, well weaned but not influenced by any adverse outside factors. In Britain the natural breeding season for budgerigars runs from late spring to autumn, so unless they are being especially bred indoors for exhibition purposes, there are unlikely to be many babies available during the winter months.

Contacting a budgie breeder in your local area is best; look for advertisements in newspapers, on the internet, check out your local cage bird society, ask friends and neighbours if they know of budgie breeders.

Never buy a baby budgie without seeing it, despite any assurances from the advertiser that it is 100% ok. There may be baby budgies for sale in pet shops, but they are likely to have been there for a few days, or possibly weeks, which negates the importance of obtaining a baby bird as soon after it has left the nest and is self-supporting.

A baby budgie can still be called a baby, and in many respects still looks like a baby, until it is about 3 months of age, when it undergoes certain plumage and physical changes. But search for the youngest on offer.

Bird auctions are becoming increasingly popular, many are held around the country each week. Bargains can certainly be had but buying this way is not for the inexperienced. As budgies cost only a few pounds the small saving would be unrealistic unless you know exactly what to look for. Although after reading this book you might be confident enough to try!

It is worth mentioning that you are protected by the Trades Description Act if you buy livestock through a retail outlet. Under the 'Sale of Goods' if you ask for a budgie suitable for a pet and they sell you a 5 year old hen that has come out of an aviary, the law is on your side. A well matured, female bird is highly unlikely to make a tame, talking pet and would be deemed, 'Not fit for the purpose for which it was sold.' You could certainly ask for your money back. If you purchase an unsuitable bird through a private sale, you do not have this legal protection.

Having found a supplier, visit and check them out. If the birds are housed in a clean environment, and not overcrowded, there is less chance of buying a sickly bird. A caring seller should be able to answer any queries with knowledge and confidence, and more importantly, is prepared to handle any of their stock for closer inspection. Confronted by cages full of twittering birds in many different colours, you may not know where to start. First, find out if these babies were bred in cages rather than outside aviaries. Cage bred birds are more suited for pet training because during their baby period they are likely to have had plenty of human contact, being well handled when the nest boxes have been inspected and cleaned. Budgies bred in flights will often have a wildness about them that will take up valuable tuition time to overcome.

You will need to have the knowledge to ensure that those birds you are being offered are genuine 'from the nest' babies. Body size can give little indication of age; a baby bird from an exhibition quality bloodline can be as big as an adult bird from 'everyday' stock. The essential guidelines to look for are the striations (fine black lines) that run across the dome of the head down to the nostrils and the 'necklace' of black spots around the throat. Juveniles and adults will have clear colour on the dome of the head (a circle of clear yellow on a green budgie, white on a blue.) From babyhood to about twelve weeks these stripes will gradually disappear, bit by bit, to be replaced by plain colour. The 'bib' of black spots are fragmented in babyhood, in maturity they come together to form six circular necklace spots, four complete, the remaining two on each 'cheek' are half covered by mauve cheek patches.

Full black eyes are another sign of immaturity, by the age of 3-4 months a pale ring will have developed around the pupil. A newly weaned bird will also have an area of dark colouring right on the tip of its beak.

It is far more difficult to put an exact age on lutino (red-eyed yellows) and albino (red eyed whites) budgies as they lack these helpful dark pigment guidelines. Here one needs to have some experience to note that the baby feathers do not have the intensity of colour of adults, the behaviour patterns are babyish and the voice immature. In my 38 years experience with budgerigars I have come to the conclusion that many lutinos and albinos seem to possess a nervous gene and require longer and more intensive training sessions before they settle. Although it has to be said that at the 1960 National Cage Bird Show at Olympia, London, the award for the 'Best Talking Budgerigar' was won by a lutino bird. The judge, budgie expert Philip Marsden, commented, "I was surprised to find that the winner was a lutino, as I know from experience that this variety is very often difficult to train but A. Appleby's bird was bang in form and full of talk."

The next step in your choice of a suitable bird is to try and choose one individual. For teaching to talk and to get the best results, it is necessary to settle for just one bird. You will become its substitute parent, sibling and 'friend', which the bird will 'copy.' Those babies that have recently come away from their parents will often huddle together at the bottom of the stock cage, trying to recreate the comforts and security of a nesting box, but natural curiosity will overcome this, and the birds should soon start investigating their new surroundings. Self-confidence is of major importance in any budgie that is being picked for a pet. So don't choose the one cowering in the bottom of the cage because you feel sorry for him. It may well be nervous and difficult to train. Look for any of the cheeky characters that have hopped up on the perch and appear unfazed

The top half shows two baby ('barhead') pied budgerigars with the striations across their heads and the fragmented necklace of spots. [These are about 7-8 weeks old, having lost the black tips to their beaks.] The other two birds are an adult skyblue hen budgerigar (brown cere, clear white head) and a light green cock budgerigar, (blue cere, clear yellow head.)

by the situation. Unless the birds have been well handled by the breeder, it is unlikely that you will be able to get them to perch on your hand, but, nevertheless, try this test. Poke a finger through the cage wires and watch the reactions. Pass on any bird that flutters to the bottom of the cage in a hysterical heap. Single out the birds that stay on the perch, or only move away at the last moment. And put to the top of the list any budgerigar that comes and nibbles your finger-nail!

Through selective breeding and some quirks of nature, today's budgerigars come in a wide range of colours, including blue, violet, albinos, spangles, pied, lacewing, saddlebacks and there's even a crested variety. If you have decided on a particular colour, ask the seller to catch up some you have chosen and put them into a smaller cage. Having now narrowed down your selection, you need to ascertain the birds are healthy. Budgies are hardy and suffer from few ailments. Stress situations such as being parted from siblings, moved around to a new location or fed a different diet, can sometimes cause tummy upsets. An ailing bird is a problem you do not need, so check the birds in your selection are 'bright-eyed and bushy-tailed.' A poorly bird sits with its eyes closed, drooping tail, soiled feathers and is uninterested in what is going on around it. If there are a number like this, it is best not to buy from this outlet as there may be infection in the stock. The feathers should be shiny, tight and clean, the birds interested, even when still huddled in a babyish heap in the corner of the cage.

Get the seller to pick up a bird from your selection and open out one of the wings. There should be a full batch of feathers with no gaps. A disease that often escapes detection, causing permanent loss of wing and tail feathers, is commonly known as 'French moult.' Although not life threatening, the bird can be left looking unsightly, and more importantly, will probably never to able to fly properly. Don't fall for the old stories that 'the bird is having a bad moult' or, 'the feathers got knocked out when the bird was being caught up.'

Look at the area around the vent. Tummy upsets will frequently soil and stain feathering on the stomach. Often dark green in colour, this could be a sign of diarrhoea, or worse, enteritis, a potential killer. Budgies which show these tell-tale signs of illness need isolating and instant veterinary attention sought.

Check the bird's beak. Does the top mandible curve neatly over the bottom one? Some birds develop beak deformities which are difficult to correct and can cause feeding problems in later life. One common cause is brought about by an over enthusiastic mother bird eagerly stuffing her chicks with regurgitated food, a 'goo' that not only goes into babies mouths but is plastered around their faces. This dries to a cement like finish, which if not quickly removed, will prevent the base structure of the beak growing correctly. The end result can cause the top mandible to become stunted and the bottom one to overgrow it. Fluffy feathering around the face can easily mask this problem in its early stages. If not corrected in time, the bottom mandible will grow continuously and can only be kept in check by careful clipping back by a veterinarian experienced in bird care.

Ask to see the parents, as there is a contagious and disfiguring disease called 'scaly face' which can affect many parrot type birds. This is caused by a small burrowing mite that gets under the skin in areas around the face, vent, legs and into the bone of the beak. The visible crusty evidence of their existence will be the dead mites that have been pushed up to the surface. Passed from bird to bird by direct contact, babies in the nest can catch 'scaly face' from infected parents whilst they are still being fed. The disease starts out as small, grey, flaky spots that are impossible to see on an infected baby bird. Left unchecked, over a period of months the scales will develop into deep, tissue-disfiguring itchy scabs, which, in advanced stages, can cause severe beak deformities and feather loss around infected areas. Fortunately, vets can treat this problem;

a popular method is to dab spot –on- the neck drops containing non-toxic, bird formulated, Ivermectin, or special creams can be bought in pet care outlets. In caring establishments with good animal husbandry, the above mentioned problems are unlikely to occur.

Male Or Female?

A baby cock bird is preferable to a hen; male budgies, in the main, possess cheerful dispositions, with more natural vocalisation and behaviour patterns that are so advantageous for pet training and talking. Some, but not all, female budgerigars, once matured, at about 6-8 months, become hormonally driven and lose interest in being a pet and instead follow their natural urge to build a nest and reproduce. Wooden perches and sandpapers at the bottom of the cage are often chewed to pieces, and if the bird has the freedom of a room, she may end up stripping off small lengths of wallpaper or tearing up magazines.

All of this can be accompanied by a change of temperament; many become so possessive they will defend 'their' cage from all comers, often inflicting nips to anyone brave enough to try and gain access. The end product of all this fussing may be a number of infertile little white eggs. According to the depth of interest, these will either be used as footballs and kicked around the cage, or optimistically sat on in the hope they will hatch out.

It has to be said that hen birds with a lower sex drive will often make affectionate, talkative pets, but few will reach the talking talents of a male bird. Author and bird lover Catherine Hurlbutt, in her book, 'Adventures With Talking Birds' states, "the females are usually dismissed as possessing little talking potential; nevertheless, there are many instances of female budgies that talked very well."

However, having worked her way through three unresponsive females, she passed the fourth hen bird onto another bird lover, whose family soon had Juliet talking. Starting with the two easiest, a wolf whistle and "Pretty bird" she continued, "this young lady was soon giving adequate versions of both, although her voice was very small and she included a good deal of gobbledygook in her efforts. Next came her name, 'Juliet,' which after much debate with myself, I had selected with the devious reasoning that if she learned to say, 'Oh Romeo! Romeo!' it would be obvious to any listener that the bird was female and her name was Juliet. She also took artistic licence with Waldteufel's 'Skaters' Waltz,' her talking sessions liberally sprinkled with its tinkling notes but she did not become a distinguished linguist. Her imitations have favoured nonhuman sounds, such as Tippy's [family dog] bark and the tapping of typewriter keys. Her voice was weak, but proof that a female budgerigar can talk."

The only behavioural difficulties cock birds may develop, when in breeding condition, is to either try and mate with, or regurgitate seed onto, a favourite toy or mirror. This can give the impression that the bird is being sick, but as long as he is bright and chirpy, this is natural behaviour. Removal of these items may solve the problem.

Adult budgerigars are easy to sex; in most colour varieties, the fleshy pad around the nostrils, called the cere, is blue for a male, brown for a female. In baby birds, both sexes have ceres of almost identical mauve-pink colour, but there is a finite difference. Baby cock birds have ceres of uniform colour, whilst the females may have a thin creamy ring around each nostril. In youngsters of around 10-12 weeks the difference becomes more obvious, but at this age, valuable training time has been lost. Males also tend to have a more domed shape to the front of their skull.

In cases of some babies where a visual difference is almost impossible to detect, I use the 'bite test.' Definitely not for the faint- hearted, but extremely effective. Hen budgies of any age are feisty and when forcibly picked up will nip the nearest piece of human flesh and squawk loudly. A baby cock bird will usually just gently nibble a finger and vocally complain more quietly.

When it comes to the value of your new pet, don't think that a more expensive, exhibition type bird will make a better pet. It will not. As long as it is of the right age, preferably male and healthy, an ordinary 'pet quality' one will do nicely. The age is the critical factor. And limit your choice to just a single bird. Any other budgies, whether in the same cage or within earshot may prove to be too much of a distraction.

Choosing A Cage

Having finally chosen your budgie, you will need a cage to keep it in. Most modern cages are well made from easy to clean materials and designed with the bird's comfort in mind. For a happy pet it is best to buy the biggest one you can afford, preferably with horizontal wires, to make it easier for the bird to climb around. But, we are talking here about a large cage, not a mini-aviary. To have fun with your budgie you need to have it within reaching distance of your hand when you open the cage door, otherwise pet training reaches stalemate.

I prefer to see wooden perches used rather than the unnaturally thin plastic variety that come with modern cages. Wood is a natural material, so well washed small branches of about ½" wide, picked from unsprayed apple or pear trees, are ideal. The varying sizes give the bird's feet useful exercise and the twigs double up as much enjoyed nibble sticks. Food and water dishes that can be accessed from the outside of the cage by the bird's owner are preferable, as this is more hygienic set up, droppings are less likely to end up in them.

The cage should be kept in a temperate room, and, for ease of access for both cleaning and training, placed at about waist to face level. Hung up too high and the bird will be exposed to unhealthy, hot, stale air. Definitely do not put the cage on a window-sill or in direct sunlight. Birds cannot sweat and can quickly suffer from heatstroke. Other potential dangers are fumes from overheating Teflon coated pans; air fresheners; household aerosols; cigarette smoke; petrol and carbon monoxide fumes.

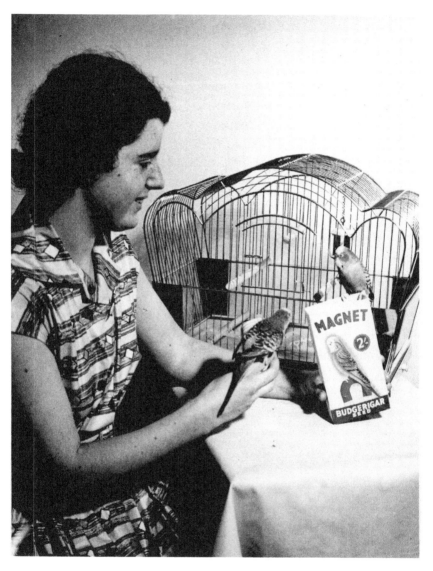

*The Author with two of her famous talking Budgies
advertising Budgerigar Seed*

Feeding

You will need to buy a suitable, clean, quality budgerigar mixture, and, as mixtures vary in their contents, find out what your bird has been fed on, buy a starter quantity from the breeder and continue with this for a week or so. Although in their natural state budgies live in dry, arid regions of Australia, and drink very little water, it is essential to offer fresh water every day. Even a well-designed, partly covered container cannot keep out airborne dirt and dust, and as the fluid warms up to room temperature, it becomes less wholesome when bacteria begin to multiply.

Some dedicated bird owners go the extra mile and only give their stock boiled water. It follows that because budgies digestive system is not made to cope with much fluid, any green food, such as lettuce, should be offered in limited amounts. Too much, and diarrhoea can result. Slices of apple are a great favourite but, if shop bought, make sure you take off the peel as it may contain preservative chemicals. Other foods they enjoy, but in small quantities, are carrot, cucumber, sunflower and sesame seeds. NEVER offer bean sprouts, chocolate, plums, lemons or potatoes, these can be hazardous.

You will also need cage bird sand (not builder's sand) or sandpapers, as suitable covering for the cage tray, with a sprinkling of bird grit on top. Budgies have no teeth so the rough grit helps with the assimilation of seed, breaking it down in the bird's crop to a digestible form. It is a natural action for the bird to forage on the ground for grit. But this can alternatively offered in a small separate dish. Most birds love millet sprays (seeds harvested on a stem) and there are essential mineral blocks and calcium rich cuttlefish which they like to nibble on. Tonics, conditioners, and other treats that the seller may recommend can be included on your new pet's shopping list.

Right now toys can wait. A baby bird will have enough to cope with, having been separated from its parents and siblings, moved into different stock cages and then being caught up and moved yet again to a new home containing a bewildering array of bright coloured objects that rattle, ring or roll around.

The First Days

N ow it is time to make your final choice and take your new pet home. It is kinder to transport him in a small cardboard box (you can buy these in your local pet care outlet or the breeder may supply one) rather than in the cage. The bird might hurt himself on the wirework if he flutters around. A compact, enclosed carrier will keep him steady and the darkness will give a feeling of security.

Once home, set the cage up as advised and, besides putting seed in the food bowl, scatter some extra grains on the cage floor. Gently tip the bird out of the box, don't try to grab him out of the container. He may crouch, bewildered, on the tray for minutes, or even hours, so if he is feeling hungry the food is near. But don't worry if he doesn't eat for the first day, many do not. Budgies only consume the seed kernels so you can tell if your bird has started to feed by the presence of the discarded dry outer husks.

Having provided all its creature comforts it is best to leave the baby bird completely alone for at least 24 hours to settle in. Everyone in the household should go about their daily business. As the cage will need cleaning out, ideally on a daily basis, and fresh seed put into the dishes, a gentle introduction to training may be started the next day. Budgies have a high metabolic rate, which means they burn up energy quickly, so even if the cage is not freshened up new seed must be added each day to ensure food is always available. Birds often put the empty husks back in the food dish, giving the impression it is still full. A small puff will blow them away, revealing edible grains underneath, which can then be topped up. Every 2-4 days tip the whole lot out and start with a fresh pot of seeds. Drinking water needs to be changed each day. Once a week give the whole cage a thorough clean, scrub the perches, wash the toys, feeders and drinkers and wipe down the soiled cage wires in a well diluted solution of disinfectant.

By the following day your baby budgie should be up on a perch and taking an interest in his surroundings. He may chirrup a little, although much of the initial vocalisation will probably be strident call notes as he tries to contact his siblings. The voices of garden birds may also set him off, causing him to run excitedly along the perches in the hope that one of his family is nearby. But after a few days he should settle down and indulge in natural behavioural traits such as stretching, preening, fluffing, shaking his feathers, yawning and napping.

Training

The first stages of training and contact will be through the daily cleaning routine. Budgies are creatures of habit so feed him about the same time each day. Early evening may well be the best time as the bird will have 'wound down' from the day's activities and should be more receptive. Talk to him whilst you are filling up the dishes, it doesn't matter what you say, just let him get used to the sound of your voice and your presence, build up a rapport. Once the bird appears to be gaining confidence, start a finger training routine. A baby budgerigar obtained a few days after weaning is often instinctively tame, seeking contact with an 'adoptive parent.'

Try tickling the top of his head or the back of his neck. This imitates the mutual behaviour of social preening and may have a calming effect. If he panics, just hold back and stay still. It will not be long before he welcomes this attention. Start finger training by gently pushing an extended finger against the front of its legs, this should persuade the fledgling to step on and hopefully stay there. If he gets flustered and dashes away in panic, just slowly and quietly withdraw your hand and try the same procedure at the same time the next day. At this stage do not be tempted to let the bird out of the cage to fly around the room. This will undo all the initial bonding work.

When the baby bird happily steps onto your finger without hesitation, and you can transfer him from perch to perch, and this should be in a matter of days rather than weeks, you have successfully got over the biggest training hurdle. In theory, if he comes willingly to you inside the cage, he should do the same outside. The time you decide to let him out, pull over the curtains so he does not fly into the glass, which he may not see, cover or remove any hazardous objects such as lighted candles, open fires, unlidded fish tanks, large water filled vases, and

Finger Training, a vital step

this includes excited children and the cat. As an extra safety precaution, the door could be locked during training time.

Repeat the 'stepping onto an extended finger' routine and when the budgie willingly steps on, gently withdraw your hand from the cage. The bird is likely to do one of three things – sit tight and feel secure, flutter onto the nearest object that seems suitable as an alternative perch, or it will make a mad dash circuit around the room.

Whatever happens, stay calm. Do not force the bird to make any hasty decisions. It is a big step for a little budgerigar coming out of its cage for the first time and every one reacts differently. Just stand still and see what he does. He may choose to walk up your arm and sit on your shoulder. If he flies and settles somewhere, or panics, quietly go over and encourage him to step onto your finger. If you have bonded well he should oblige and you can then put him back into his cage.

Any bird that plays up needs a longer period of training in the confines of the cage. Getting into a regular routine of letting the bird out at the same time will help him learn what to expect. Budgies are incredibly intelligent and will quickly work things out for themselves.

Never be tempted to clip some of your baby bird's wing feathers to prevent him flying. A few bird tutors recommend this, saying that it will prevent the budgie from hurting itself if it flies all over the place in a panic. I personally feel this is depriving the bird from behaving in a natural way and causes it to become stressed.

Toys

P lay toys can be introduced as soon as you feel your new pet has settled. There is a fantastic choice on the market, all of which will give the budgie much playtime pleasure, from ladders and swings to mirrors and imitation budgies that clip on the perch. Whether to put a mirror in the cage is debatable; some bird trainers feel such a 'companion' toy gives comfort and confidence to a baby bird, others believe their pet is more responsive to training without one; some birds can become so besotted with the image they lose interest in the training programme.

Budgie toys!

Do not, though, overload the cage with so many playthings that the bird can hardly move around. Give him about half a dozen a time, keep the surplus in a box and periodically change them.

Although not truly a toy, you can buy bird baths which will either hang on the cage door opening or can be placed in the bottom of the cage. Budgies are not natural bathers, but many enjoy splashing around and their plumage will have that extra shine from the ablutions. A bird that is wary of getting wet can often be tempted into the water by putting in a small piece of lettuce or dropping in their favourite toy. Any budgie that refuses to get its feet wet can occasionally be given a gentle spray instead.

A Budgie Playstand being appreciated

Teaching To Talk

Although much of the attraction of budgerigars is in the pleasing range of beautiful colours, their ability to mimic adds so much to their pet appeal. They do not possess a larynx like us, so their production of words and intonations is restricted to a somewhat squeaky voice.

Women and children with their higher pitched voices appear to have more success than males at teaching budgies to talk. The timbre of one person's voice may be more appealing to the bird and the results more successful.

Clear enunciation is a must; regardless of how much talent your bird may possess, his abilities as an avian linguist will depend mostly upon your performance as a trainer, especially if you can tap into your pet's psychology and character. Some budgies will happily respond to a variety of trainers, where each may utter interesting speech features that the bird finds irresistible and wants to copy, especially if it is delivered in a theatrical fashion. And a pet that talks will often go on to master casual household noises, such as barking dogs, sneezes, or a bit of a tune that appeals to him.

There are many training tapes available that can be played to encourage bird mimicry, or you can simply record your own chosen words and play them for about ten minutes a couple of times a day. But don't overdo repetitive training tapes, otherwise your bird may get bored. And don't use those with different voices as the bird may then become confused. Recording the tutoring sessions can often be beneficial; by playing them back, your pet may well develop an interest in furthering his vocabulary, encouraged by what he has heard.

But nothing beats the close, loving contact between owner and pet. As with finger training, teaching to talk may often have greater success if done in the early evening when the bird is settled and therefore more responsive. There is no quick way to get results, but the more bonding time you can spend with your budgie the better the results will be.

Some owners find that simply sitting by the cage and repeating a single word, such as "Hello" or the ever popular "Pretty Boy," may soon show results; there is much to be said for covering the cage with a light cloth during these 'lessons', then the bird has no distractions.

Other trainers encourage the bird to sit on their hand, to be brought up near their mouth until feathers touch lips, the vibrations from this close contact can be a successful alternative method. Although it has been known for the occasional curious budgie to try to climb inside their trainer's mouth to find out where the sounds are coming from!

Try 'building budgie bridges' by attempting to copy your pet's own language, of clicking, tutting and trilling sounds. Budgies are colony creatures, therefore it will begin to be drawn in and feel that is becoming a member of the household, thus developing the natural instinct to communicate. It will therefore become physically and emotionally fulfilled.

The first few attempts at mimicry may not be uttered with clarity, the sounds bundled into the bird's natural chatter, but constant tutoring will encourage the budgie to fine tune its efforts. Always be patient, don't get frustrated or annoyed, the bird can pick up the feelings and become unsettled. Playing some relaxing music during training periods is a tip used by some successful trainers, but turn off the distracting TV. A really settled budgie will often perch on one leg, and a truly contented one will make 'crackling' noises with his beak, the avian equivalent of a contended cow lying down in a meadow and chewing the cud.

Amusing as it may sound, read a bedtime story to your pet; it just gets him more into hearing the sound of your voice. When he does finally come out with that first word, praise him and give him a small reward, say a small sprig of millet. Of

Close contact can be beneficial

course, he won't understand the words of praise, it is how they are uttered, the intonation, the emotions he can feel and tune into.

Once the first few words have been mastered, you can progress onto sentences, taught in segments, teaching the first half and, when mastered, adding the second half. Train him to say his name and address in case he ever gets out and becomes lost. Keep a notebook by the cage to record your pet's speaking progress, listing the words he likes and the ones he doesn't. I have found that budgerigars willingly learn to talk until they reach the age of about a year.

Again, individuals do vary, but they do seem to become less responsive as they reach adulthood. There is no magical, quick way to get your bird to talk, but the more bonding time you can spend with your pet, the more productive his vocabulary should become.

Complications

Never be tempted to keep two birds together in the hope that they will both talk. Although not impossible, this is unlikely to happen; they will be far more interested in each other than in the trainer. Even if you get one bird to talk, and then introduce another, their interest in mimicry will usually wane.

Although it is rewarding to have a tame, talking budgie, it must be said that they do not understand the meaning of the words they copy. Some words come about by association; "Goodbye" uttered as someone leaves a room or "Hello" as they enter, but they do not have the same meaning to the bird as they do to us.

For budgies that appear disinterested in attempting to talk, an article by Mrs. V. Farrup in an archive issue of 'Cage and Aviary Birds' suggests that a change of scenery might do the trick. She wrote: 'I never imagined that a budgerigar would enjoy a long journey by car and boat, but when my husband and I returned from Germany with Sammy, our 18-month–old pet, he stood up to the travelling exceedingly well and enjoyed every minute of the trip. Although normally not a great talker, he chatted to his plastic toy bird almost non-stop. Even on board ship he continued to talk and he has continued to do so ever since our arrival in England, coming out with many words we have never heard him repeat before. My advice to anyone who has a lazy talker is to take their bird for a change of scenery; he will enjoy the break as much as you will.' Putting the bird in another room could encourage a more positive response.

Another contributor to the same magazine, Miss A. O'Driscoll, wrote: "I bought a budgie from a pet shop. It was a delicate looking pale blue bird which seemed to spend most of his time in a huddle on the floor of the cage. I felt a bit anxious about him and thought he probably would not live very long. My sister was sorry for him and spent some time each day looking at him and saying "Poor Georgie." One morning, a few weeks later, a little voice came from the cage, "Poor Georgie." The budgie had apparently been suffering from a type of depression. Things have altered since then, as we now have a healthy budgerigar, with quite a large vocabulary, which includes, "It is nice to see you" and "Do take your coat off and have a cup of tea," which delights our visitors."

Some of the most common reasons why a budgie will not talk:-

The first chosen word was too difficult.

The training time is too short.

He can hear other budgies.

Too many people trying to teach him.

Too much always going on around him.

Hasn't bonded well enough with his teacher.

And – with too much enthusiastic tutoring, he simply might not have been able to get a word in edgeways!

I hope that I have been able to give you some useful guidelines which will result in a tame, talking pet that melts your heart. Remember, keeping budgies should be fun, they are only small but have big personalities and give so much in return.

Enjoy.

My National Cage Bird Show Winners In The Talking Bird Classes

1959 2nd in Talking Parrot section. 'Lulu'. Yellow Fronted Amazon.

1960   BEST TALKING PARROT. 'Lulu'.
Judge bird expert Philip Marsden commented: "Elizabeth Wright's Yellow Fronted Amazon was really quite unquenchable with her imitations and was a good winner."

1961 BEST TALKING PARROT. 'Lulu'.
Judge Charles Trevisick from Ilfracombe Zoo commented: "The winner was Elizabeth Wright's Yellow Fronted Amazon, the best talker I have found for several years."

1962 2nd. 'Lulu'.

1963 BEST TALKING PARROT. 'Lulu'.
Judge Charles Trevisick commented: "Miss E. Wright's Yellow Fronted Amazon parrot was an easy winner and probably the best Amazon that has been here for a couple of years."
3rd. 'Lollipop'. Blue Fronted Amazon parrot.
Judge's comment: "A fair talker."
5th. 'Cocky'. Lesser Sulphur Crested Cockatoo.

1964. BEST TALKING PARROT. 'Lollipop'. Blue Fronted Amazon.
Judge Percy Edwards commented: "A clear winner on the day."
2nd. 'Lulu'.

3rd. 'George'. Yellow Fronted Amazon parrot.
6th. 'Cocky.' Lesser Sulphur Crested Cockatoo.
4th. 'Sparkie'. In Talking Budgerigar class.

1965. 2nd 'Lollipop'. Blue Fronted Amazon.
Judge's comment: "Lollipop is a very nice steady Amazon
parrot and was not far behind the winner."
4th. 'Cocky'. Cockatoo.

1966. 4th. 'Lulu.'
5th. 'Lollipop'.

Wins between 1959 and 1966
4 x 1st. 4 x 2nd. 2 x 3rd. 3 x 4th. 2 x 5th. 1 x 6th.

Some Clever Talking Budgerigars

PIP-PIP

Little Pip-Pip, a light green budgerigar, put his talking abilities to good use when he flew out of the window of his owner's home and got lost. Barmaid Ruth Durbin found him perched in a tree at the bottom of her garden. As he hopped onto her hand he said, "I'm Pip-Pip, I live at number seven Strawberry Close, Nailsea, got that? Who's a clever boy then?" He was reunited with his owner, retired factory worker, Arthur Bendon, who said: "Trying to get him to say Strawberry Close was difficult, he kept saying Sodbury Close at first. I spent months teaching him his name and address, just in case something like this happened."

SPARKIE WILLIAMS

Acknowledged as probably the best talking budgie ever, was Sparkie Williams. Hatched in 1954, at Houghton-le-Spring, he was a baby green budgie bought at the age of 6 weeks by Mrs. Mattie Williams, who called him Sparkie because "He was a bright little spark." Mattie has been described as 'a childless housewife with a husband, a perm, string of pearls and large framed glasses. But the devotion from this elderly lady for her adored pet was obvious, under her caring tutoring and careful enunciation, within three weeks he'd picked up "Hi Puss" and "Pretty Sparkie" and quickly learnt his name and address, because, as Mattie said, "This was just in case he got lost."

Her Geordie accent was exquisitely duplicated in "Mama's prrrecious birrrd, mama's little treasure, I love my mamma," and his voice was once described as 'sounding like that of a middle-aged woman from Newcastle playing a polite Dalek.' She tutored him every day, and in 1958, when he was three and a half years old, he won the BBC International Cage Word Contest. He was so good he beat 3,000 other chatterers, but was disqualified from ever taking part again as the judges felt there was never going to be a budgie good enough to beat Sparkie.

From this little Sparkie found fame; he was courted by bird seed companies and was signed up for two years to front an advertising campaign for Caperns bird seed, and made a 7in Flexi disc with Mattie to help the Caperns customers to teach their birds to talk. He appeared on the BBC's Tonight programme with Cliff Michelmore, and his most ambitious enterprise was the record by Parlophone a 78rpm where 20,000 records were made, running time 8 minutes, where Sparkie is in conversation (edited) with world budgie expert Philip Marsden.

An amusing record was made with Lorrae Desmond, called 'Sparkie the Fiddle' where the bird is 'playing the part' of an American gangster with Lorrae as his girlfriend and partner in crime. This recording was so popular it was regularly requested on radio programmes 'Housewife's Choice' and Family Favourites.'

At the age of eight years Sparkie started to ail; as he lay dying Mattie cupped the feathery bundle in her hands, blowing on him in the hope that the warmth of her breath might keep 'her baby' alive. His last words were 'I love you Mama.'

During his life it was claimed that Sparkie had acquired a vocabulary of 531 words, could say over 300 sentences and recite 10 different nursery rhymes, earning him a place in the Guinness Book of Records. Being no ordinary bird, and a much loved and treasured pet, Mattie had him preserved and mounted on a perch by a premier taxidermist. He has had a musical tribute to his life; an hour long opera, 'Sparkie: Cage and Beyond' composed by Michael Nyman, which played to packed audiences at the Haus der Berliner Festspiele, at the MaerzMusik festival in Berlin on the 26th March 2009. Author Andrew Dodds wrote a book 'I, Sparkie, World

Famous Champion Talking Budgerigar.' And stuffed Sparkie finally ended at up at the Great North Museum - Hancock at Newcastle.

JOEY COMPTON

Joey (Joby) Compton is a handsome three year old pied cock budgerigar with an extensive vocabulary that ranges from "You plonker, Rodney" and "Talk to me nicely" to "Put the kettle on" and "You little stinker."

Mike and Sue Compton had kept a couple of budgies before, and when they saw an advertisement for some baby birds being offered for sale in the local area they decided to buy one.

Their friend Mrs. Kempshall had given them some expert guidelines:

She wrote 'If you want your budgie to talk, you should get a very young cock bird, as they make the best talkers. The bird should have left the nest only a few days, but must be able to feed himself. Before talking lessons begin the bird must be tamed. First teach him to stand on a pencil or a thin strip of wood and later on your finger. Make all your movements slow and deliberate. Hurried movements will only frighten your little pet. It will not be long before you can rub your nose up and down his breast feathers and tickle the back of the budgie's neck. Taming will be taken up to a month. Then you can teach the budgie to talk. Attempt only one word at a time. This word should be spoken clearly and near to the bird. The next word will be easier and so on, until you can teach him sentences. As a rule, women make the best teachers because their voices are clear and light.'

Mike said, "We went and saw the breeder and asked for a baby cock bird for a pet. He had large indoor breeding cages and showed us three six week old babies that were ready to go. Sue originally fell for one that was lavender blue but the breeder pointed out that it had a slightly deformed foot." So they decided to buy Joey instead and "When we brought him

Joey

home he sat in the bottom of the cage, he never ate, he never had a drink that day and we thought we had bought the wrong one. We were really worried. So we got him out, held him in our hands and offered him a few grains of seed, which he ate. He loved being held, you could even turn him upside down, and then he'd go to sleep snuggled in our cupped hands. He especially enjoyed it when we held him, tickled his tummy and head and rocked him to sleep. But he won't let you do it now."

They started to teach him to talk straight away with the ever popular "Pretty Boy." Sue said, "I repeated those words until I was sick of saying them. I never said anything else to him and within ten days he'd got it. We never move on to a new word or phrase until he has completely mastered the one we are teaching him. There are certain sentences he's not interested in mimicking; he can do a brilliant cough or laugh and we've said many times in response 'That's not funny' but he's never copied that. Some things he will pick up very quickly, such as when he's sitting on the top of his cage we've said "Are you on guard then?" He goes to my sister when we are on holiday and I'll guarantee he'll come back with a batch of new sayings, the latest being, 'Och aye da noo'."

Even at the age of three, Joey still keeps adding to his repertoire which now runs to well over 100 items. These include:

It's a bed time, night night sleep tight, see you in the morning.

Be a good boy.

Put the kettle on.

I give you a kiss (mwa)

What the time, it's ten to nine.

Who's my beautiful boy?

Stop that noise.

Easy Peasy Lemon Squeezy.

Who dares wins.

For goodness sake.

Silly sausage.

I beg your pardon.

What a load of rubbish.

Hello mate.

Simples.

Come and see your Dad.

Cheeky chops.

Mummy's gone shopping.

Joe Joe wants a cuddle.

Lovely jubbly.

Other Talking Bird Species

Apart from budgerigars there are many other varieties of birds capable of mimicking the human voice. Probably the best are Greater Indian Hill Mynah birds; their enunciation and tonal quality, along with their jaunty nature, produce as near perfect an imitation of the human voice as any bird can manage. Following in vocal ability are African Grey and Amazon parrots, macaws, cockatoos, various parakeets and cockatiels. Rooks, crows and magpies can say a few words and it is on record that a hand reared canary and a bullfinch could also copy the human voice.

The three hundred and fifty members of the parrot family have been kept as talking pets for centuries, certainly since the days of Ancient Greece, and possibly before. Legend has it that Hannibal, on his famous trek across the Alps in 218 BC took along not only his war elephants, but his favourite talking Indian ring-neck parakeet.

Many of the red-tailed African greys have superb memories and are able to retain an extensive vocabulary. Sir Winston Churchill, Marie Antoinette and Henry VIII have all kept these birds of brains and beauty.

For many years Prudle, a male belonging to Mrs. Lynn Logue, of Golders Green, London, was listed in the Guinness Book of Records as the world's most talkative bird. His ability to imitate appeared unlimited; he could utter over 1,000 sayings and won the Best Talking Bird Award at the National Cage and Aviary Birds Exhibition for twelve consecutive years. His party piece was to hang upside down from the top of his cage, swing backwards and forwards, shouting, "I'm a tick-tock, I'm a tick-tock."

Indiscretion by African grey parrot Ziggy led to the parting of the ways for Chris Taylor and Suzie Collins. As they snuggled up on the settee, Ziggy shattered this domestic harmony by uttering, in Miss Collins' voice, "I love you Gary," followed by loud kissing noises. The unidentified Gary turned out to have been a frequent secret visitor.

Steve Nichols from the National Parrot Sanctuary in Lincolnshire said that some of his 756 unwanted birds "utter language so foul that it is worse than you would get on a building site." An Amazon parrot called Paco, had learnt a great deal of filthy language, much of it unrepeatable, but "Oi, fat arse, shift" and "I'll get you, you fat cow," being two of his milder utterances. One feathered resident loved to shout at passing women, "Get your knickers off!" Another talented bird could whistle the Eastenders signature tune, followed by "Not that bloody programme again." Steve added, "The speed at which African greys pick up sounds and language is quite unbelievable. I now have to change my mobile ring tone every two days, if I don't, the parrots will learn it and I find myself running around the sanctuary looking for my phone before realising its fifty parrots playing games with me."

Geoff Grewcock, from the Warwickshire Wildlife Sanctuary in Nuneaton quickly discovered that Barney, a seven-year-old blue and gold macaw had picked up some ripe Anglo-Saxon language from his previous owner, having told the Mayoress on a civic visit to "F*** off," then turned to the vicar and two police officers and added, "You can f*** off too, w******!" Said Geoff, "I knew that Barney could swear but what has now happened is shocking, because he has been teaching our two African greys these choice words when we had our backs turned. It sounds like a builder's yard with all the abuse flying about. They just sit there swearing at each other."

Crows, rooks, magpies, jackdaws and ravens are all highly intelligent birds with conspicuous personalities and imitative talents. Their natural vocabulary consists not only of "caws" but a wide range of other sounds. In his book, 'Birds of the World,' Oliver L. Austin explains that crows 'have mental ability of a high order…with patience captive ones can be taught to say a few words.'

Author Katherine Hurlbutt writes in her book, '*Adventures with Talking Birds*' that 'although mockingbirds of the south-western USA are accomplished mimics of other birds' songs, they rarely include human sounds in their repertoire, even when in contact with human voices. I have only ever uncovered one authentic report of a wild mockingbird that talked. The mocker's territory included a property owned by a man named Edward. Apparently Edward's wife called him so often that the bird picked up the word.'

One cheeky Amazon green parrot in a pet shop would bid customers a cheery "Good-bye, bye-bye" as they headed for the door. Her mimicry was so spot on that the departing persons were fooled into thinking it was a member of staff speaking and responded in like fashion. The bird would then yell "F… off", followed by a mad cackle of laughter.

One of the most unusual talking birds was Butch, a hand-reared bullfinch, which lived in the aviary of Terry Greening, a Teignmouth cab driver. He said, "I couldn't believe my ears when, aged sixteen months, Butch started saying 'Who's a pretty boy then?' I've never heard a finch talking in all the twenty years I've kept birds." His wife, Jean, always greeted the bird and his thirty other avian companions each morning at feeding time with a few whistles and kissing noises and she said, "I always say to him 'Who's a pretty boy then' just as a greeting, I wasn't trying to train him because I thought it was impossible for him to mimic voices, but he just picked it up. He speaks three or four times a day, usually in the morning. We whistle to each other as I hang out the washing. I think he's trying to stretch his vocabulary now because it seems he's trying to say, 'Birdy, birdy, birdy', which is how Terry greets the birds."

Who's a Chatty Boy Then?

And the last words have to go to Sparkie Williams…

"I'm just a little bird,
But I can talk and chatter all day.
Nursery rhymes plainly can be heard.
I'm a clever little budgie, aren't I, eh?"

…and from Joey Compton

"Have a nice day, God bless you."

--ooOoo--

We hope you have enjoyed this book and found it useful.

Please visit our Facebook page, https://www.facebook.com/talkingbudgie, and share your experiences of training your budgerigar to talk.

If you have found this book useful, please review it on Amazon, www.goodreads.com and other websites. Reviews help to inform others about the book and help to pass on the message of how to keep budgerigars happy and loved.

Happy training your Budgie!

Who's a Chatty Boy Then?